ST. CHARLES YOUTH MINISTRY
The Church of Tomorrow
... And Today!

CHRISTIAN INITIATION
OF OLDER CHILDREN

Sandra Figgess, R.S.C.J.

CHRISTIAN INITIATION OF OLDER CHILDREN

Illustrated by
Mary Lou Winters, F.S.P.

A Liturgical Press Book

THE LITURGICAL PRESS
Collegeville, Minnesota

Christian Initiation of Older Children is a fully revised and integrated edition of *Preparing Older Children for Baptism* published in 1988.
The prayer over the water (pp. 15) and the welcoming words (pp. 36) are from the *Rite of Christian Initiation of Adults* copyright © 1985 International Committee on English in the Liturgy Inc. All rights reserved.

Christian Initiation of Older Children was first published in the United Kingdom by St. Paul Publications, Slough.

© St. Paul Publications 1990. All rights reserved. This edition for the United States of America and Canada published by The Liturgical Press, Collegeville, Minnesota 56321.

ISBN 0-8146-2103-1

4   5   6   7   8   9

Contents

Introductory notes

The RCIA for children of catechetical age

This booklet is intended to help unbaptized children of catechetical age to prepare to become full members of the Church with the help of a parent.

With the introduction of the *Rite of Christian Initiation of Adults* the sacraments of Christian initiation – Baptism, Confirmation and Eucharist – have been brought back together again and the Church is encouraging the practice of celebrating all three sacraments on the same day for children as well as for adults. This practice emphasises the unity of the three sacraments. The stages of becoming a Christian are not those represented by three different sacraments of initiation but rather by the three stages of the RCIA:

- The Rite of Welcome into the Order of Catechumens
- The Penitential Rites
- The Sacraments of Initiation (Baptism, Confirmation, Eucharist).

These rites can be found in chapter 5 of *Rite of Christian Initiation of Adults*.

When an infant is baptized it is the parents who take full responsibility for fulfilling the baptismal promises. When an adult is baptized the responsibility is that of the baptized person. But a child of catechetical age is in an intermediate position. The child must ask for Baptism but can only do so with parental support and consent. The child must know something of the Christian tradition and have some understanding of the commitment that is being made, but it should also be understood that the child is entering upon a process of catechesis which does not end with the sacraments of initiation.

The arrangement of this booklet

The first section of this booklet explores the meaning of being a Christian under the title *On becoming a Christian*. The first chapter of this section is structured around the blessing of the baptismal water and the central rite of Baptism. The second chapter looks at the gifts of the Spirit and the Christian's call to help build the kingdom of God. The third chapter explores the meaning of the Eucharist.

The second section, entitled *The way to become a Christian*, explains the various preparatory and explanatory rites surrounding the act of Baptism as well as looking more closely at the sacrament of Confirmation and the reception of the Eucharist. The booklet follows here the three steps on the way to full sacramental initiation as they are described in the *RCIA* and explains the meaning of the symbols and rituals that are used.

While Baptism is the central sacrament in Christian initiation, it is the Eucharist which is at the centre of the continuing Christian life. There is therefore a chapter which looks at and explains the various moments of an ordinary Sunday Mass and emphasises that regular participation in the Eucharist is necessary to sustain the New Life received in Baptism.

Section two should be used at the appropriate points in the child's journey to sacramental initiation – that is, as immediate preparation for the three moments of the rite. The main core of the catechetical material is in Section One. This should be studied after the child has been received into the Order of Catechumens and before the other stages. The last chapter might be used as part of the post-baptismal catechesis.

The material in this booklet

The material in this booklet has been used with children between the ages of 5 and 13. Younger children will need a great deal of parental help, and it would be appropriate to use a well illustrated Children's Bible for the Bible stories referred to in the text. Older children are able to work much more independently and may prefer to use a good, up-to-date translation of the Bible.

While the material is primarily intended to help children of catechetical age who are preparing for Baptism it could also be used to help children baptized in infancy to understand what was done for them when they were too young to remember and so to prepare for the completion of their own Christian initiation through their First Communion.

A Bible or (for younger children) a Children's Bible and a notebook are needed in addition to this booklet. The last chapter also requires a Missal.

Section 1

ON BECOMING A CHRISTIAN

1
The meaning of Baptism

WATER

Water in Baptism

When you are baptized, the priest or deacon pours water over your head. In the early years of the Church, most of the people who were baptized were grown-ups. They were taken down to a river and baptized in deep running water. They went right down under the water. The water came over their heads and then they came up again and took a great gulp of fresh air.

Water in everyday life

Think of at least six ways in which we use water in everyday life. *Write them down in a notebook and draw some pictures to show how much we need water.*

Can you think of any ways in which water is dangerous to us? *Write these down in your notebook as well.*

Water is so important to our lives that it speaks to us of LIFE itself. But because it is also dangerous, it can also speak to us of DEATH.

Prayer of blessing of the baptismal water

Holy Saturday night is a very special and holy night. On this night the Church, that is, the people of God, wait together to prepare for the great happiness of Easter Sunday. And while we wait, we remember. We start right at the beginning and remember God's goodness in making the world. We remember the long time of waiting and preparation before Jesus came. And we remember God's promise to give us life together with him for ever.

Holy Saturday night is a special time for Baptism. If someone is baptized at this time it helps all the rest of us to remember that all of us are called to rise to a new life together with Jesus Christ.

The baptismal water is blessed during this night. And the priest uses this prayer:

> Father,
> you give us grace through sacramental
>   signs
> which tell us of the wonders of your
>   unseen power.
> In baptism we use your gift of water,
> which you have made a rich symbol of
>   the grace
> you give us in this sacrament.
>
> At the very dawn of creation
> your Spirit breathed on the waters,
> making them the wellspring of all
>   holiness.
>
> The waters of the great flood
> you made a sign of the waters of baptism

that make an end of sin
and a new beginning of goodness.

Through the waters of the Red Sea
you led Israel out of slavery
to be an image of God's holy people,
set free from sin by baptism.

In the waters of the Jordan
your Son was baptized by John
and anointed by the Spirit.

Your Son willed that water and blood
    should flow from his side
as he hung upon the cross.

After his resurrection he told his disciples:
"Go out and teach all nations,
baptizing them in the name of the Father,
    and of the Son, and of the Holy Spirit."

Father,
look now with love upon your Church
and unseal for it the fountain of baptism.

By the power of the Spirit
give to this water the grace of your Son
so that in the sacrament of baptism
all those whom you have created in your
    likeness
may be cleansed from sin
and rise to a new birth of innocence
by water and the Holy Spirit.

The celebrant before continuing touches the water
with his right hand.

We ask you, Father, with your Son
to send the Holy Spirit upon the waters of
    this font.

May all who are buried with Christ in the
    death of baptism
rise also with him to newness of life.

We ask this through Christ our Lord.

We are going to look closely at this prayer
because it reminds us of some of the stories in
the Bible which talk about water.

WATER IN THE BIBLE

> 1. "At the very dawn of creation your Spirit breathed on the waters, making them the wellspring of all holiness."
>
> (*Cf. Genesis 1*)

This reminds us of the story at the very beginning of the Bible in the Book of GENESIS, chapter 1. This story tells us how God breathed the Spirit upon the waters and created the world.

Find the story in your Bible. In your notebook, draw or paste in pictures of some things that make our world so beautiful.

Remember that God created all this beauty by breathing the Spirit upon the emptiness. THANK GOD for all the beautiful things God has made in our world.

In your notebook write down a THANK YOU *prayer to God.*

Here is a very ancient "thank you" prayer of the Church which you should learn by heart:

> Glory be to the Father,
> and to the Son,
> and to the Holy Spirit.
> As it was in the beginning,
> is now
> and ever shall be
> world without end. Amen.

> 2. "The waters of the great flood you made a sign of the waters of baptism that make an end of sin and a new beginning of goodness."
>
> *(Cf. Genesis 6)*

This story comes from the Book of Genesis, chapter 6. *Find the story in your Bible.*

The story tells us that God was so saddened and disappointed by the way that people treated their beautiful world, that God started all over again. Water is used here to destroy. It is used to bring DEATH. But God saves NOAH and his family and enough animals and birds to start again. After the flood LIFE begins again. There is a fresh start and the RAINBOW in this story is a promise of God's love.

(a)   Think of some of the things in your own life which spoil the beauty of God's world and hurt other people. Tell God that you are sorry for these things. Ask God to help you make a new beginning. Here is a prayer that you might use:

> Dear God, our maker,
> thank you for loving us all so much
> and for helping us always to begin again.
> I am sorry for the times that I have hurt
> my family and friends
> and spoiled your beautiful world.
> Please forgive me and help me to love you
> more. Amen.

Try writing your own prayer of SORROW *in your notebook.*

(b)   Can you find pictures of places where there have been disasters – floods or earthquakes or war? *Put them in your notebook.*

PRAY for the people who are suffering like this. Ask God to help them make a fresh start and find new life and new hope. Ask God to remember the promise of the rainbow and show love especially to those who most need God's help to start again.

Write down your prayer in your notebook.

> 3.   "Through the waters of the Red Sea you led Israel out of slavery, to be an image of God's holy people, set free from sin by baptism."
>
> (*Cf. Exodus 14*)

This story comes from the Book of Exodus, chapter 14. *Find the story in your Bible.*

The people of Israel were slaves in Egypt. God chose MOSES to be their leader and to take them away from Egypt to their own country where they could be free and happy and serve God. But the Pharaoh who ruled over the Egyptians would not let them go. Every time that the Pharaoh said "no" to Moses when he asked him to let the people go free, God sent a plague upon the Egyptians. Finally Pharaoh was so fed up that he let the people go. But when they had set off on their journey, he changed his mind and set off after them with soldiers. When they reached the RED SEA, Moses prayed to God to save them. An amazing miracle took place: the waters of the Red Sea parted and the people of Israel walked across the sea. But when the Egyptians tried to follow, the waters came back over them and they were all drowned.

Jewish people always remember this story as a sign of God's great love for them. They remember that God set them free and looked after them in their need. God SAVED them.

And we go on telling the story because we believe that God also loves us and sets us free.

Answer these questions in your notebook:

(a) What do you think it means to BE FREE?

(b) Some of the things that stop us from being free come from outside ourselves. Can you think of countries where people are not free to be themselves and to serve God? Pray for these people. Ask God to show them love.

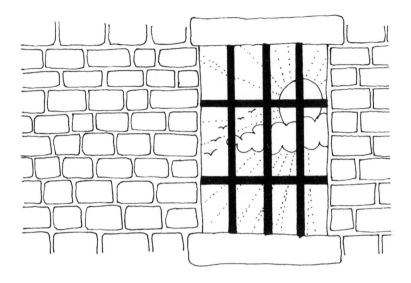

(c)   But some things that stop us from being free are inside ourselves. This is what we call "sin". It includes our bad habits, our meanness and our unkindness – all the things we said "sorry" to God for in the last prayer. These things hurt other people but they also hurt us and prevent us from being free to love and serve God.

* How do you think that Baptism sets us "free from sin?"
* How does this story make you feel about the Egyptians?

When the Jewish people remember this story they think of the Egyptians with sadness. They empty a little wine out of their glasses because the Egyptians who were also God's children had to suffer.

Jesus teaches us that we should love our enemies:

> "Love your enemies and pray for those who persecute you."

These words can be found in the *Gospel according to Matthew*, chapter 5 verse 44.

- Is there anyone you should pray for like this?

> 4. "In the waters of the Jordan your Son was baptized by John and anointed by the Spirit." (*Cf. Mark 1*)

You can find this story in the *Gospel according to Mark*, chapter 1.

The River Jordan flows right through the land of Israel. It is the river that makes the land fertile so that food can be grown there.

Trace a map of Israel into your notebook and mark in the Jordan River.

Jesus was baptized by going right down under the water. When he came out of the water, God sent the Holy Spirit to show that Jesus was God's beloved Son.

Jesus was baptized just before he began his life's work or ministry.

God gave this special sign to show that God

was pleased with everything Jesus would say or do.

When you are baptized, you are called a son or daughter of God and you also have something very special to do. You are called to share God's love with other people and help them to know about Jesus.

How can you find out more about Jesus so that you can help to spread the GOOD NEWS?

> 5. "Your Son willed that water and blood should flow from his side as he hung upon the cross." (*Cf. John 19*)

Read the story of the arrest, trial and crucifixion of Jesus in the Gospel according to John, *chapters 18 and 19.*

St John tells us that while Jesus hung on the cross one of the soldiers pierced his side with a spear and that at once *blood* and *water* poured out. When we Christians remember this story, we think of *blood* and *water* as signs of LIFE, the life which Jesus gave up for us because he loved us so much.

All through his life Jesus showed love for people by the things that he said and did. And he didn't just love some people. He loved all people:

> He loved poor people and rich people;
> He loved sad people and happy people;
> He loved good people and "bad" people;
> He loved friends and strangers;
> He loved men and women;

He loved grown-ups and children;
He loved clever people and simple people;
He loved short people and tall people;
He loved thin people and fat people;
He loved black people and white people;
He loved everyone.

In your notebook, collect pictures from magazines or make drawings to show all the different kinds of people that Jesus loves.

• How should you feel about all these people if you are going to be a follower of Jesus?

Jesus' love for all these people made some of the rulers angry. *Look again at your Bible. Find out the names of some of the people who were angry with Jesus.*

• Why do you think the rulers wanted to get rid of Jesus?

• How do you think that Jesus felt about the people who plotted to put him to death?

ASK GOD to help you understand how much God loves YOU – just as you are. And ask God to help you to love other people better.

Write down your prayer in your notebook.

---

6. "After his resurrection he told his disciples: 'Go out and teach all nations, baptizing them in the name of the Father and of the Son and of the Holy Spirit'." (*Cf. Matthew 28:19*)

Jesus died on the cross. But after three days HE ROSE FROM THE DEAD. God's power was so strong in him that death could not hold him. His rising from the dead shows us that:

LIFE is stronger than DEATH
LOVE is stronger than HATE
GOODNESS is stronger than EVIL
LIGHT is stronger than DARKNESS.

Read the stories in your Bible, especially the Gospel according to John chapters 20 and 21, that show how Jesus appeared to his friends after he rose from the dead and comforted them.

- How do you think they felt when Jesus appeared to them?
- Were they happy? Scared? Confused? Comforted? Hopeful?

When they got over the shock, the friends of Jesus found that they had been given something special to do, a message to spread around the world.

Read the message in Matthew's Gospel, chapter 28 verses 16-20.

- What are they asked to do?
- What did they have to tell people?

Part of the task was to baptize those who believed in Jesus and wanted to follow his way of life. Now let's think about that for a moment. Do you remember that baptism in the early days meant going right under the water and coming up again? And do you remember that water speaks of LIFE and DEATH? Just as Jesus died and rose again, so the followers of Jesus copy him using water to act out DYING and RISING to new LIFE. By doing this they act out the belief that:

LIFE is stronger than DEATH
LOVE is stronger than HATE
GOODNESS is stronger than EVIL
LIGHT is stronger than DARKNESS.

THE IMPORTANCE OF NAMES

In the last section we read that the disciples were to baptize in the NAME of the Father and of the Son and of the Holy Spirit. When you are baptized you are baptized by NAME.

Your name

Your name is very special to you.
It marks you out as a person in your own right.
It marks you out as being different and special.

You are baptized by NAME to show that God loves YOU for the person that YOU are. God doesn't just love you along with a crowd of other people.
God knows you by name.
God knows all about you. Jesus said even the hairs on your head are counted!
And God loves YOU. Especially YOU.
In the Bible there are many stories of God calling people by name. Often God gives them something special to do. Sometimes God even changes their names to show more clearly what God is asking them to do.

Find out about:

- Abram whom God called and re-named ABRA-HAM (*Genesis, chapter 17*).
- SAMUEL whom God called by name in the night (*1 Samuel, chapter 3*).
- Simon whom Jesus called and re-named PETER (*Matthew, chapter 16*).
- Saul who had a vision on the road to Damas-cus and became PAUL (*Acts, chapter 9*).

The name of Christian

Jesus called his friends one by one and called them each by name. But he never asked them to "go it alone". He wanted his friends to look after one another and to help one another to bring his message to the world.

So when you become a Christian you do not have to follow Jesus on your own. You join a great family of people who are all called by the name of CHRISTIAN. And this family is called the CHURCH.

Before you are baptized you are introduced to this new family by name. And this, your new family, welcomes you and promises to help you and to pray for you.

God's name

People have sometimes believed that to give other people your name is to give them power over you – to give them some hold on you. Some people don't like to give their names.

If you have a person's name you can report that person to the police if there is a reason to do it, or you can spread nasty stories about that person. On the other hand you can also spread good news about a person whose name you know. You can pray for him or her. You can call him or her and invite that person to visit you.

So, for God to give the chosen people God's name was an act of trust and love.

In your Bible, in the Book of Exodus, *chapter 3, read the story of how God spoke to Moses from the burning bush and told him the name of God.*

The Jews called God by the name YAHWEH, the name which Moses learned from the burning bush. But the name was so holy that they never pronounced it out loud.

Jesus taught us a name for God. He taught us to call God "Father".

In the name of the Father

When we call God "Father" we are saying that we believe in God's love for us. God's love is strong and tender and caring like the best love of our mothers and fathers, only better.

We are also saying that we believe God is the source of our life. God gives life to us and to the whole world. And God takes care of all our needs.

Here are some of the things which Jesus taught us about the Father:

- Your Father knows what you need before you ask him.

- When you pray, don't use a lot of words or make a show. Go to your own room and your Father will hear what you have to say to him secretly. And he will answer you.

- If you forgive others their faults, your Father will also forgive you.

- Look at the birds. They don't sow or reap or store up food but your heavenly Father feeds them. And he loves you even more.

- Your Father in heaven makes his sun shine on bad people as well as good and gives rain to the honest and dishonest.

You can find all these sayings in the SERMON ON THE MOUNT (*Matthew, chapters 5 and 6*).

Make sure that you know the prayer which Jesus taught us to say:

> Our Father,
> who art in heaven,
> hallowed be thy name;
> thy kingdom come;
> thy will be done on earth
> as it is in heaven.
> Give us this day our daily bread
> and forgive us our trespasses
> as we forgive those
> who trespass against us;
> and lead us not into temptation,
> but deliver us from evil.

And of the Son

- JESUS is the only SON of the FATHER
- He is the only Son of GOD.

But he invites us all to become sons and daughters of God. We do this by taking on his name in Baptism – the name "Christian" – and by living in the way that he has taught us.

We become children of God in Baptism. But we have to go on becoming more like Jesus all through our lives.

We need to learn more about him.
We need to learn to talk to him.
We need to learn to listen to him.
We need to meet other people who are also
    trying to become more like Jesus so
    that we can help one another.

Read some more stories about the life and teachings of Jesus. After each story, write down in your notebook one way in which you can become more like Jesus.

Here are some of the many stories you might read to learn more about Jesus:

Name of Story	Something it tells us about	Where to find in the Bible
Jesus heals a man with a useless hand	Jesus is never afraid of what people might think	Mark: ch. 3 vv. 1-5
Jesus heals a little girl	Jesus goes on believing even when others laugh	Mark: ch. 5 vv. 21-43
Jesus forgives Zacchaeus	Jesus has time for the people no one else wants to know	Luke: ch. 19 vv. 1-9
Jesus feeds the crowd	Jesus can use even little gifts to do great things	John: ch. 6 vv. 1-14
The prodigal son	Jesus teaches that the Father never gives up loving us	Luke: ch. 15 vv. 11-32
The good Samaritan	Jesus knows that the most unexpected people can be our friends and helpers	Luke: ch. 10 vv. 25-37
The widow's penny	Jesus cares more about how we give than how much we can give.	Luke: ch. 21 vv. 1-4

And of the Holy Spirit

Read the story of the day of PENTECOST (*Acts, chapter 2, verses 1-18*).

The followers of Jesus were all shut up together in a room with locked doors. They were waiting "for what the Father had promised". They had already been given a job to do – they were meant to go out and tell all the world about Jesus and that he had risen from the dead.

But they were far too uncertain to do anything about it. And then something happened to them. The HOLY SPIRIT came into their hearts and made them strong and brave and very sure that Jesus was still with them.

The Holy Spirit is the POWER and LOVE of God at work in our lives. The Holy Spirit helps us to become more like Jesus. The Holy Spirit helps the Church to carry on the work of Jesus – to share with all the people the love that God has for us.

When you are baptized you are given the Spirit of Jesus so that you can share in God's LOVE, WISDOM and STRENGTH.

And when you are confirmed, the Church prays that the Holy Spirit may always be your helper and guide. We pray that you may be wise and brave and full of love for God.

SUMMING UP

When YOU are baptized

in WATER,
by NAME,
in the name of the FATHER
and of the SON
and of the HOLY SPIRIT,

YOU BECOME

– a child of God the FATHER
who is able to grow
more like Jesus the SON,
through the power of the
HOLY SPIRIT who lives in you,

– and a member of the Christian family,
the CHURCH.

WELCOME TO THE FAMILY

When you are baptized you become a member of the Church. You belong to that great family of people from all over the world who call upon God as "Father" in the Christian's family prayer.

There was a time when only baptized Christians were allowed to say the "Our Father". It was a family secret! And so the "Our Father" which we say together at your Baptism is very special.

It is the first time that you say "Our Father" as a full member of the family.

And when you say "Our Father" you join together with your brothers and sisters in every country of the world, in every known language. You join together with all those people whom Jesus loves:

rich and poor
sad and happy

good and "bad"
friends and strangers
men and women
grown-ups and children
clever and simple
short and tall
thin and fat
black and white.

All these people are now your brothers and sisters. So let them all say to you:

We welcome you joyfully into our
    Christian family,
where you will come to know Christ better
    day by day.
Together with us you will try to live as
    children of God,
for our Lord has taught us: "Love God
    with all your heart
and love one another as I have loved you."

Looking more closely at the family prayer

Our Father,
who art in heaven,
hallowed be thy name;
thy kingdom come;
thy will be done on earth
as it is in heaven.
Give us this day our daily bread
and forgive us our trespasses
as we forgive those
who trespass against us;
and lead us not into temptation,
but deliver us from evil.

- Notice that we call God "OUR FATHER" and never MY Father.
  If we call God "Father" together, what should we call one another?
  How should we treat one another?

- HALLOWED BE THY NAME means that we want to love and honour God and we want everyone everywhere to know how good God is.

- THY KINGDOM COME, THY WILL BE DONE means that we want things to be done God's way, in our own lives and in the world around us.
  How do you think the world would change if God's will was done everywhere on earth?

- GIVE US THIS DAY OUR DAILY BREAD.
  After we have prayed first for God's will to be done, we turn to our needs.
  We ask God to give us all the things we need for today.
  BREAD stands for all that we need, not just food; but also clothes and friends and, above all, God's own presence with us.

- FORGIVE US AS WE FORGIVE.
  God promises to forgive us but God makes a condition that we forgive one another.
  TRESPASSES is an old-fashioned word meaning sin.

- LEAD US NOT INTO TEMPTATION, DELIVER US FROM EVIL.
  We ask God to protect us from all that could harm us or turn us away from God.

Getting to know another member of the family – and another prayer

MARY, the mother of Jesus, is a very special member of the Christian family.

- She is the first Christian.
- Mary was the first to believe in Jesus.
- Mary was the first to give Jesus to the world.

Because we also believe in Jesus and we are also called to bring Jesus to the world, we find in Mary, the woman who believed, an example, a helper and a friend.

Read the story of the ANNUNCIATION in your Bible (Luke, chapter 1 verses 26-35).

Ask Mary to help us to obey God as she did.
Christians like to call on Mary using the words of the angel. We ask her to pray for us and so we say:

> Hail Mary, full of grace,
> the Lord is with thee.
> Blessed art thou among women,
> and blessed is the fruit of thy womb,
>   Jesus.
> Holy Mary, mother of God,
> pray for us sinners,
> now, and at the hour of our death.
> Amen.

2

Building God's kingdom together

When we say the Lord's Prayer, we pray: "Thy kingdom come...". All the time that Jesus was preaching and teaching he kept telling people that the kingdom of God was very near. And all of us who follow Jesus are called to work together to build that kingdom. To build God's kingdom we need the help of the Holy Spirit.

At your CONFIRMATION the Church prays that the Holy Spirit may always be your HELPER and GUIDE. We pray that you may receive all the gifts of the Holy Spirit to help you live as a Christian and to help to build God's kingdom.

This is the prayer the bishop or priest says as he holds out his hands over you in blessing:

All-powerful God, Father of our Lord
    Jesus Christ,
by water and the Holy Spirit
you freed your sons and daughters
    from sin
and gave them new life.
Send your Holy Spirit upon them
to be their helper and guide.

Give them the spirit of wisdom and
    understanding,
the spirit of right judgment and courage,
the spirit of knowledge and reverence.
Fill them with the spirit of wonder and
    awe in your presence.
We ask this through Christ our Lord.

Gifts for a king

In your Bible, find Isaiah chapter 11 verse 2. Can you find the same gifts mentioned here as in the prayer? The translation may be a little different but try to match up the different names for the same gifts. Write them down in your notebook like this:

Confirmation Prayer   Isaiah 11 in my Bible

   Wisdom
   Understanding
   Right judgment
   Courage
   Knowledge
   Reverence
   Wonder & Awe

When the prophet ISAIAH wrote this verse the people of Israel had a bad king who did not honour God and did not look after the people. Isaiah PROPHESIES that one day there will be a truly good king who will love God and will really care for his people. He will be fair to everyone and will care for:

     rich people and poor people
     sad people and happy people
     good people and bad people
     friends and strangers
     men and women
     grown-ups and children
     clever people and simple people
     short people and tall people
     thin people and fat people
     black people and white people.

This king will bring peace and happiness so that even the wild animals will live together in friendship and the whole world will be at peace.

Read Isaiah, chapter 11 verses 6–9, and in your notebook make a drawing or paste in pictures to show Isaiah's prophecy of a world of peace and friendship.

Quite soon the people of Israel did have a much better king who tried to honour God and to care for all the people. But Christians believe that Isaiah's prophecy only really came true when Jesus was born. Jesus Christ is the only King who really rules in the power of the Spirit with:

Wisdom
Understanding
Right judgment
Courage
Knowledge
Reverence
Wonder & Awe.

Jesus is the only King who can bring justice for all people and true peace.

Isaiah's prophecy came true in part with the birth of Jesus. And each one of us can know Jesus Christ as the wise and loving King of our lives who can bring us peace. But the prophecy is also still about the future. We still do not see the "wolf and the lamb lying down together". We still see plenty of fighting in the world. We still find people quarrelling with one another – even in our own families, even in the Church itself. We still find that poor people are not treated with justice. We still have a long way to go until the earth is a place of true peace and justice.

The building bricks of love

When you are confirmed you are being asked to play your part in helping to build God's

kingdom of justice and love. This is why the Church prays for you on the day of your Confirmation, that you may receive the gifts that are needed by a good and just king.

It is not easy to know the right way to act at all times and this is why you need the kingly gifts of

Wisdom
Understanding
Right judgment
Courage
Knowledge
Reverence
Wonder & Awe

to help you make choices which are good and which help to make peace and true happiness.

These gifts are not really separate from one another. They all work together because they all grow out of the same spirit of trust in God and love for one another.

So much sadness and suffering in the world comes about because we are afraid of one another and do not understand each other. And when we do not trust one another it is very difficult to act in a way which is wise and just.

• Can you think of times when you have been afraid of someone and have acted unwisely?
• Can you think of times when you have been unkind to someone you do not understand?

When we love God we learn to REVERENCE all that God has made and to treat God's creation with WONDER and AWE rather than with fear. In this way we learn to respect one another.

Our trust in God gives us COURAGE to overcome our fear. And when we are no longer afraid we can come to UNDERSTAND one another.

When we see one another with the KNOWLEDGE that comes from love we can make RIGHT JUDGMENTS in WISDOM.

It is only by growing in this spirit of love and trust that we can help to build God's kingdom on earth.

Look at Mark chapter 12 verses 28-34.

- What does Jesus say is the first of all the commandments?
- And what is the second?
- Why does Jesus say to the scribe: "You are not far from the kingdom of God"?
- Is it possible to keep the first commandment and not the second?
- How can you try in your life to put these two commandments into practice?

Look at Galatians chapter 5 verses 22-23.

- Write down the fruits of the Spirit listed in this verse.
- Try to explain the meaning of some of the words in this list. (You could draw or cut out magazine pictures or tell a story to show what these words mean.)
- What difference will it make to the people around you if your life shows the fruits of the Spirit?

Look at Acts chapter 2 verses 32-37.

- Why were there no needy people among the believers?
- How should we as Christians treat the things that we own?
- Can you think of some small way in which you can share something you own with somebody who has less?

Look at 1 Corinthians chapter 13.

This is one of the most beautiful passages in the Bible and it is a description of love. Read it out aloud slowly and let the words sink in to you.

Perhaps you could learn some of these verses by heart. Come back to this passage often as a reminder of the way of love which you are trying to follow as a Christian.

Confirmation and the Eucharist

When you are baptized into Jesus Christ and confirmed with the Holy Spirit you become a full member of the family of the Church. And this means that you can share fully in the family feast of the Eucharist. Up until this time you have been present at Mass but you have not been invited to receive Communion. And in the early days of the Church the CATECHUMENS (who were the people learning to be Christians who were not yet baptized) were not even allowed to be present for the second part of the Mass. But when you are confirmed you will be able to take a full part in the Mass. And so we must go on to think about the meaning of the family feast.

3
The family feast

Eating together in friendship

In the Gospel story we hear over and over again
about Jesus eating and drinking with other people.
Sometimes he was the host. Sometimes he was
the guest. Some of those who sat at table with

him were important and respected people. Some were poor and despised people whom others did not want to know. Sometimes there was a feast. Sometimes it seemed there was not going to be enough food for everyone.

Here are some of the meals the Bible tells us about:

Mark: ch. 2 vv. 15-16	Jesus eats with tax collectors and sinners
Mark: ch. 6 vv. 39-44	Jesus feeds 5000 people from five loaves and two fishes
Luke: ch. 14 vv. 1,12-14	Jesus eats with a Pharisee and teaches him to invite the poor to his table
Luke: ch. 19 vv. 1-10	Jesus is a guest at the table of Zacchaeus
Luke: ch. 7 vv. 36-50	Jesus eats with Simon the Pharisee and allows a "bad" woman to anoint his feet
John: ch. 2 vv. 1-11	Jesus goes to a marriage feast and turns water into wine
John: ch. 12 vv. 1-3	Jesus eats with Martha and Mary at Bethany

Good and pious people in Israel at the time of Jesus were very careful about sharing meals with the "right" people. Only those who kept all the religious laws could sit at their tables. And a good and religious person would never think of being a guest at the house of a "sinner". These good people who kept all the rules were called PHARISEES. They believed that they were pleasing God by keeping away from ordinary people who could not keep the rules so well. They believed that the way to make God's kingdom come was to keep all the rules perfectly and to stay away from "sinners".

- Why do you think that eating together with someone is so important?
- When we invite people to our homes why do we usually invite them for a meal or at least for a drink?
- Are there people whom you would not want to eat with? Why?

Jesus shocked the Pharisees because he invited everyone to his table and was ready to be a guest in any house. He knew that God's kingdom was for everybody and not just for a few. Jesus showed God's love and acceptance for everyone by eating together in friendship. And while they ate together Jesus talked to them about God's love and forgiveness. He told them stories to teach them about the kingdom of God. Some of the best loved parables are stories that Jesus told to explain why he shared food and friendship with "sinners".

Find Luke chapter 15 in your Bible. Read the story of THE PRODIGAL SON *in verses 11-32. Then look at verses 1-3.*

- Why do you think Jesus told this parable?
- Does it help to explain why Jesus ate with "sinners"?
- Some religious people were shocked that Jesus spent so much time at parties. Does this story give any answer?

The friends and followers of Jesus still like to listen to his stories and to feast together with him. We do this now by being together at Mass and sharing the Communion Bread and Wine.

Jesus is with us now just as much as he once was with his friends in Israel. And the key to how this can be is in the very last meal that Jesus shared with his friends on earth.

The Last Supper

The night before Jesus died was a special feast for the Jews. It was the time when they remembered together the great moment in their history when God saved them from slavery. *Look back to page 21 and remind yourself of the story of the Exodus from Egypt.*

Even today Jewish families gather together on Passover night to tell the great story of God's love for them. The youngest child asks the question "Why is this night different from all other nights?" And the oldest person present tells the whole story – how God saved the Israelites from the power of Pharaoh and brought them safely across the Red Sea. In order to help make the story come alive, the story teller points to the special Passover symbols on the table and says something like this:

> *Pointing to the lamb bone* – "This bone is a symbol of the lamb whose blood kept the Israelites safe on the night that the angel of the Lord 'passed over' the homes of our ancestors."

> *Pointing to the unleavened bread* – "Why do we eat this unleavened bread now? It is because our ancestors did not have time to let the dough of the bread they made for the journey from Egypt rise."

> *Pointing to the bitter herbs* – "These bitter herbs remind us that our ancestors suffered bitterly when they were slaves to the Egyptians."

> *Pointing to the Charoseth* (a *mixture of grated apple, honey and spices*) – "This Charoseth is to remind us of the mortar from which our ancestors had to make bricks without straw."

> *Pointing to the salt water* – "And this salt water is to remind us that God brought us out safely through the Red Sea."

This is the Passover message: in every generation, including our own, each one of us must look upon ourselves as if we had been delivered from Egypt. It is not just our ancestors whom God saved from slavery. It is we ourselves whom God is saving even now.

When Jesus celebrated the Passover with his closest friends he did something new and unexpected. He used a new symbol to show his friends that he was giving his life for them. He showed them how they must die so that they could share more closely and fully in his life and discover God's saving love in a new and even more wonderful way.

He took a loaf of bread and broke it and shared it out. Until the loaf was broken it was separate and apart from the disciples around the table. But when it was broken and shared out and eaten it became part of their bodies. And those who had eaten the bread were now linked together. The loaf had become a part of them.

In just this way Jesus gives himself to us. Because he gave his life for us, he is no longer separate and apart from his friends. He gives himself to us. He becomes part of us. And as we feed together on the bread which is his body we become part of his body. We are made one with him and we are made one with one another.

This is what Jesus meant when he took bread and broke it and said:

"This is my body which is given for you. Do this to remember me."

(*Luke 22:19*)

53

This is what the priest means at Mass when he takes the host and says:

"Take this all of you and eat it:
this is my body which will be given up for you."

This is what the first Christians meant when they said:

"The bread which we break, is it not a sharing in the body of Christ? Because there is one bread, we who are many are one body for we all share in the one bread."

(*1 Corinthians 10:6-17*)

At the Last Supper, Jesus also took a cup of wine. He shared this with his friends saying:

"This cup is the new covenant in my blood which is poured out for you."

(*Luke 22 :20*)

At Mass the priest still takes wine and says:

"Take this all of you and drink from it:
this is the cup of my blood,
the blood of the new and everlasting covenant.
It will be shed for you and for all
so that sins may be forgiven.
Do this in memory of me."

Jesus is telling his friends through the wine the same thing that he has already said with the bread. His death on the cross brings us much closer to him and to one another. He is now going to live with us and in us. His life can be shared with his friends because his blood has been poured out for us. He is as much part of us as the wine that we drink. And because we all drink together from the same cup we are also brought close together. This is a new way of living. It is a new COVENANT or promise from God. This new covenant is made possible by the dying and rising again of Jesus.

Jesus used these new symbols of bread and wine at a Passover meal. This shows us that in the death and resurrection of Jesus God has done an even better thing for us than God did for the Israelites by bringing them out of slavery in Egypt. When the Jews celebrate the Passover they remember God's special love for them as a people who suffered a great deal and who have known God's love to reach them in their suffering and to bring them new joy and new hope. When we celebrate the death and resurrection of Jesus we remember God's love for all people. And because Jesus has died and risen again we know that God is with us and suffering with us in all the pain and sadness of human life and this gives us the strength to go on living with hope and love. We know that:

LIFE is stronger than DEATH
LOVE is stronger than HATE
GOODNESS is stronger than EVIL
LIGHT is stronger than DARKNESS.

When the Jews listen to the Passover story they know that they are sharing in the story that they remember: "It is not just our ancestors whom God saved from slavery. It is we ourselves whom God is saving even now." And so it is that every time we come to Mass we share again in the saving love of God made known to us through the life, death and resurrection of Jesus. It is not just Peter, James and John, Mary Magdalen, Zacchaeus, and Martha who knew the freeing love of Jesus. It is we ourselves who today are loved and made free through Jesus who is with us still.

The Eucharist

The other name for the Mass is the EUCHARIST. This is a word which means thanksgiving. The Eucharist is the great prayer of thanksgiving to God for all that God has done for us. At the Eucharist we remember and give thanks for all that God has done for us from the very beginning. We give thanks for the beautiful world which God has made. We give thanks that God still cares for the earth and for all living things. We give thanks for God's love made known through the history of God's people. We give thanks that we are invited to know and love God and that God renews that invitation over and over again. And above all we give thanks for the great love that God has shown us through the death and resurrection of Jesus.

At the Eucharist we are invited to sit at table with Jesus just as his friends did in Israel. We are invited to listen to his stories through the Bible readings. We are invited to remember that God loves us always and that God wants us to love one another. We are invited to sing and to be happy together in the presence of God.

But at the Eucharist we are also invited to come closer to Jesus and to one another by eating the bread which is his body and by drinking the wine which is his blood. By coming closer to Jesus in this way we can grow to become more like him.

At the Eucharist we are invited to pray together that God's kingdom will come on earth. We are invited to give strength and courage to one another by coming together and showing that what none of us dares to do alone we can do together. We are the body of Christ because we share together in the bread which is his body.

Becoming more like Jesus

Do you remember that

- in Baptism you become a child of God the Father who is able to grow more like Jesus the Son through the power of the Holy Spirit who lives in you?

- and in Confirmation the Holy Spirit comes in a special way to be your helper and guide?

You can only be baptized once and you can only be confirmed once. But you can go on receiving the Eucharist each week, or even each day. In this way you can grow closer to Jesus so that you can grow to be more and more like him.

Coming often to the Eucharist is one very important way of becoming more like Jesus. But the Eucharist only makes sense if we live out in our everyday lives the beliefs that we celebrate in the Eucharist.

- In the Eucharist we give thanks to God for the great gift of creation. Nowadays many people are concerned for the future of the earth. There are worries about pollution of earth and sky. How can you help to treat God's creation with respect and so show that you are truly thankful for what God has made.

- In the Eucharist we give thanks for God's kindness in feeding us and caring for us. How can you show care and kindness to those around you?

- In the Eucharist we give thanks to God who is always ready to love and forgive us. How can you grow to understand and respect those who look and speak and eat differently from the way that you do?

- In the Eucharist we give thanks to Jesus who did not go along with the crowd but spoke out for the poor and despised. Can you think of times when you may have the chance to stick up for someone who is being bullied or ridiculed?

- In the Eucharist we give thanks for the resurrection of Jesus from the dead. We celebrate our hope that God brings Life even from the worst experiences. When you are sad or unhappy, can you learn to believe that God is still with you?

Living the Eucharist in this way is not easy and we will often fall short of the beliefs that we celebrate. We do not need to be discouraged by our weakness, but we do need to encourage one another to go on trying. This is why we need to gather together often to celebrate the Eucharist and to keep our hope alive. In this way we can grow together to become more like Jesus and so be a sign of the New Life which God gives.

Section 2

THE WAY TO BECOME
A CHRISTIAN

Becoming a learner

The Rite of Welcome
into the Order of Catechumens

In the early years of the Church, the people who were preparing for Baptism were called CATECHUMENS. It is a word which means learner. Other words which belong with this one are CATECHISM (the book from which you learn) and CATECHIST (the person from whom you learn).

Try saying these words out loud until you can remember them.

In the first step on your way to Baptism the Church family welcomes you as a person who is learning how to become a Christian. You are accepted into the learner's club. This is called THE ORDER OF CATECHUMENS. And there is a special ceremony to welcome you into the Order of Catechumens.

Saying "I want to be a Christian"

Before you can join any club or group you have to say that you want to belong. And this is the same with the Church. You have to tell the people in the Church that you want to belong, that you want to be a Christian, and you want to follow Jesus Christ.

Because you are not grown up, your parents also have to say that they want you to prepare for Baptism. And all the people in church have to say that they are going to help you in learning how to be a Christian.

Signing with the cross

The sign of the cross is the special sign of Christians. The cross is the place where Jesus died for us.

During the life of Jesus the cross was a sign of disgrace and punishment. It was the place where criminals were executed. But Jesus loved us so much that he was not afraid to die a shameful death to set us free. And so the sign of disgrace and punishment has become a sign of hope and love.

The priest or deacon will make the sign of the cross on you to show you that you belong to Jesus Christ and to remind you that Jesus loves you.

He will also invite your family and friends, who also belong to Jesus, to make this sign upon you. You may also be signed with the cross on other parts of your body like ears, eyes, mouth, heart and shoulders to show that Jesus is with you in everything that you do and say.

All through your life you will go on making the sign of the cross for yourself when you "cross yourself" and say:

> In the name of the Father
> and of the Son
> and of the Holy Spirit. Amen.

Every time you make the sign of the cross like this you remember that you belong to Jesus, who loves you.

Receiving the Word of God

If you are going to learn how to be a Christian you will need to learn the Christian story. You will learn the stories about the Jewish people who waited for so long for the coming of Christ. You will learn about Moses and Abraham and King David and how they trusted in God. But most important of all, you will learn the stories about Jesus.

And so, at this ceremony where you officially become a learner or Catechumen, there will be some especially chosen readings from the Bible – the book which tells the Christian story. And if you do not already have a Bible of your own, you may be given one during the ceremony.

Turning from darkness to light

Rite of Penance

Look back to page 19 where we read the story of Noah and thought about saying sorry to God.

God loves us very much and is always ready to forgive us, even before we ask. But for our own sake we need to learn how to say sorry.

We need to learn how to ask God to help us change the things in our lives we are sorry about. And so, before your Baptism day there is another ceremony in which you come to church to accept God's forgiveness and the strength to live a life which is pleasing to God.

Some of your friends who were baptized as babies may be coming to the church at the same time to make their "First Confession". They will also be receiving God's forgiveness and celebrating God's love and kindness.

All through your life as a Christian you will need to go on accepting God's forgiveness. Sometimes we call this "Confession" (owning up to the things we have done wrong). Sometimes it is called "penance" which means making some special effort to make up for the wrong we have done. But the best name is "reconciliation" because this means making friends with God and accepting God's love for us and that is what this is really all about.

Prayer of exorcism

This is a prayer for protection. The word EXORCISM means "sending away" and in this prayer the priest or deacon sends away everything which is harmful and which could draw you away from God. He asks God to look after you and give you strength at moments of temptation.

He asks God to keep you from darkness and lead you into light.

Anointing with the oil of the catechumens

In the early years of the Church the catechumens were not allowed to come to the whole of the Mass. After the readings and the homily the catechumens would be asked to leave the church. They would go to another room to learn more about Jesus and the Church.

Sometimes there would be special prayers for catechumens. They would be anointed with oil. The people would pray to God to look after these friends who were preparing for Baptism. They asked for them to be healed and to be protected from all harm and from all evil. The oil was used as a sign of God's healing love and of God's power to fight evil.

Can you think of any ways in which we use oil in everyday life for healing or soothing? Look for advertisements in coloured magazines which show this. Put them in your notebook. Wrestlers cover themselves with oil before they fight. Can you think why they do this?

In the part of the world where Jesus lived there are many olive trees. Oil can be squeezed from the olives and this oil was used as a healing ointment as well as for cooking and for burning as a light. Oil was a very precious substance and it was fitting that it should be used as a sign of God's healing love. This oil came to be known as the oil of the catechumens.

You too will be anointed with the oil of the catechumens. The priest or deacon will again pray for you and ask God to give you strength. He will most probably anoint you on your hands. The oil he uses is olive oil and it was blessed by the bishop in a special ceremony in the cathedral on the Thursday before Easter.

(NOTE: *The anointing can take place on the day of Baptism instead of at the ceremony for Step Two.*)

Celebrating the sacraments of Christian initiation

1. Baptized into Jesus Christ

Finally you come to the day of your Baptism – the day when you become a full member of the Christian family. It is a day of great joy and thanksgiving for all that God has already done for you. And it is a day of great hope for all that the future holds for you as a follower of Jesus Christ.

Blessing of the water

The priest or deacon will first bless the water of Baptism using the same prayer that we studied on pages 15-18. *Look again carefully at the words and remember the long story of God's love for us.*

Saying "I believe"

At the beginning of your journey towards Baptism you came to church to say: "I want to belong, I want to follow Jesus Christ". Now, on the day of your Baptism, after you have grown to know and understand the story of God's love for you, you can say: "I believe".

The priest or deacon will question you. He will first ask you to promise to turn away from everything that draws you away from God.

He may say:

"Do you reject Satan
and all his works
and all his empty promises?"

And you answer:

"I DO"

SATAN is a word which means enemy and it is a way of talking about everything in the world which acts against God's loving plan. Satan is God's enemy and our enemy because everything which gets in the way of God's plan make us unhappy.

The priest or deacon will then ask you to say that you believe in God the Father who made the world, in Jesus Christ our Saviour and in the Holy Spirit. He will also ask you to say that you believe in the Church, the family of God.

Look again at pages 30-36 and at your own note-book and remind yourself of what you have learnt about God, the Father and the Son and the Holy Spirit, and about God's Church.

Baptism

You go to the font and the priest or deacon pours water over your head, calling you by your name and baptizing you in the name of the Father and of the Son and of the Holy Spirit.

Remember that when YOU *are baptized*

in WATER,
by NAME,
in the name of the FATHER
and of the SON
and of the HOLY SPIRIT,

YOU *become*

a child of God the FATHER
who is able to grow more like JESUS,
the SON,
through the power of the HOLY SPIRIT
who lives in you.
And you become a member of the
Christian family, the CHURCH.

The white garment

Remember how we said that in the beginning grown-ups were baptized in the river and went right down under the water? They were naked when they were baptized in this way. When they came out of the river, they needed to be clothed. So they were given a new white garment. The white garment was a sign of the New Life they were given in Christ.

When babies are baptized we usually wrap a white shawl around them as a sign of this New Life. *You will need to talk with your parents about the most suitable thing for you to use as a "white garment".*

The candle

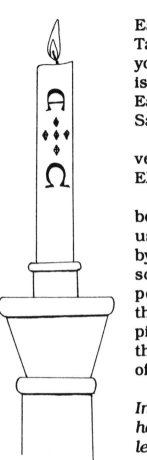

Have you noticed the big Easter Candle in the church? Take a good look at it next time you are in church. This candle is blessed each year at the big Easter Vigil celebration on Holy Saturday night.

The blessing is done with a very joyful song called the EXULTET.

In the EXULTET we remember that Jesus Christ has set us free from the fear of death by his rising from the dead. The song says that just as the people of Israel were led through the wilderness by a pillar of fire, so we are guided through our lives by the light of Christ.

In your Bible, find the story of how the people of Israel were led through the wilderness by a pillar of fire.

At your Baptism you will be given a candle which is lit from the Easter Candle. This is to remind you that you must always follow the light of Christ. And you must also bring that light to other people.

When we were baptized into Jesus Christ,
we were baptized into his death.
So by our baptism into his death we were
buried with him,
so that as Christ was raised from the dead
by the Father's power,
we too should begin living a new life.

(*Romans 6*)

Enlightened by Christ walk always as children of the light and keep the flame of your faith alive in your heart.

2.   Confirmed with the Holy Spirit

In your Baptism you receive the HOLY SPIRIT who is the POWER and the LOVE of God at work in your own life. Now, at your CONFIRMATION, the Church prays that the HOLY SPIRIT may always be your helper and guide. We pray that you may receive all the gifts of the Holy Spirit to help you to live as a Christian in the world.

Look again to pages 40 and 44 to remind yourself about the gifts of the Holy Spirit.

Laying on of hands

The bishop or priest stretches his hands out over you while he prays for you to receive all the gifts of the Holy Spirit. This gesture is known as the LAYING ON OF HANDS.

In the Bible, the laying on of hands is used as a special way of blessing and praying for someone. It is often used when someone is being asked to do something special and so needs to have extra strength and wisdom.

Here are some of the many places where you can find laying on of hands in the Bible:

Matthew: ch. 19 vv. 13-15	Jesus lays hands on the children
Acts: ch. 13 vv. 1-5	The Church at Antioch lays hands on Barnabas and Saul before sending them on a special mission
Acts: ch. 13 vv. 1-5	The apostles lay hands on seven men to prepare them to look after the needy in the Church
Acts: ch. 19 vv. 1-6	Paul lays hands on some disciples of John the Baptist after first baptizing them.

When the bishop or priest lays hands on you, he is praying that you will be blessed by God and that you will have the strength and wisdom you need to help to build God's kingdom on earth.

Anointing with chrism

CHRISM is made from olive oil – just like the oil of the catechumens, it is blessed by the bishop on the Thursday before Easter. But this time the oil has a perfume added to it so that it has a sweet smell.

Anointing with chrism has a completely different meaning from the first anointing with the oil of the catechumens. That first anointing was a preparation for Baptism and a prayer for healing. But this second anointing is a sign of your special task as a baptized Christian.

Remember how we said that in the beginning grown-ups were baptized in the river and went right down under the water? They were naked when they were baptized in this way. And when they came up, dripping wet, from the water, the first thing that happened was that they had sweetly perfumed oils poured over their heads and all over their bodies so that they shone with oil.

This was to show that as Christians they must shine with the presence of Jesus in their lives. And the sweet smell of the oil was a reminder that they must bring the sweetness of the presence of Jesus with them always.

This same oil of chrism was used to anoint prophets, kings and priests. Prophets, kings and priests all had a special job to do. You are being called and anointed to bring God to the world by the kind of person that you are and also by telling other people about Jesus.

So chrism, the sweet-smelling oil, is a sign of the attractiveness of a Christian who really follows Jesus. Your life should also attract others to follow Jesus.

Look at those colour magazines again. This time look for pictures that advertise oils and perfumes that people use to make themselves more attractive.

• How are you to be attractive as a Christian?

When the bishop or priest anoints you, he calls you by your name and says:

"Be sealed with the gift of the Holy Spirit."

While he does this one or more of your godparents or sponsors stand by you with a hand on your shoulder. This is to show that we do not have to build God's kingdom alone. On the day of your Confirmation you are being asked to do a very big and awesome thing. You are being asked to bring Jesus to the world. You are asked to make his peace a reality in your life and in the lives of those around you. But you do not have to do this alone. You work together with all those others whom Jesus loves:

> rich and poor
> sad and happy
> good and bad
> friends and strangers
> men and women
> grown-ups and children
> clever and simple
> short and tall
> thin and fat
> black and white.

It is together as one family that we are called to build God's kingdom on earth.

It is the Holy Spirit who draws us together and gives us the strength and wisdom to build that kingdom.

This is why you need to be sealed with the Holy Spirit.

3. *One in the body of Christ*

After you have been confirmed you will receive the bread which is the body of Christ and drink the wine which is the blood of Christ. You will take a full part in the Eucharist for the first time. This is also called "making your first Holy Communion".

COMMUNION is a word which means being close together with someone.

• Whom do you come close to when you receive Holy Communion?

Some of your friends who were baptized as babies may be making their First Holy Communion at the same time as you do. This will be a very special day for them as well as for you.

After the priest has said the long prayer of thanksgiving called the Eucharistic Prayer (see the next chapter for more about this prayer) he will invite you to come and receive the bread and the wine which are the body and blood of Christ. Because this is your special day, those of you who are receiving Jesus in this way for the first time will be invited to receive Communion first.

The priest will first offer you the bread. As he does so he will say:

The body of Christ.

You answer:

Amen.

You say "Amen" to show that you understand and agree that the bread you are receiving is no longer ordinary bread but the special bread which is the body of Christ. You are taking this bread to become more like Jesus. You are taking this bread because you are now a full Christian and you are part of the body of Christ.

Then the priest will offer you the cup of wine. As he does so he will say:

The blood of Christ.

And you answer again:

Amen.

You say "Amen" to show that you understand and agree that the wine which you are drinking is no longer ordinary wine but the special wine which is the blood of Christ. As we drink together from this special cup we come closer to Jesus and closer to one another. We are in communion with Jesus and in communion with one another.

After you have received Communion you will have a little time to thank God quietly in your own words for all that God has given you on this very special day when you have been

baptized into Jesus Christ,
sealed with the Holy Spirit,
and fed with the body and blood of Christ.

Now you are fully a member of the Church which is the Body of Christ. Day by day you will grow to know Jesus better. You will learn to love God with all your heart and to love others as Jesus has loved you.

You can only be baptized and confirmed once. But you can make your Baptism more and more alive by coming often to the Eucharist. Every week you can receive the bread which is the body of

Christ and the wine which is the blood of Christ. In this way you can grow to become more like Jesus and help to share the Good News of God's love for all people.

> I thank my God whenever I think of you; every time I pray for you all, I pray with joy remembering how you have helped to spread the Good News. My prayer is that your love for each other may increase more and more... and you will reach the perfect goodness which Jesus Christ produces in us for the glory and praise of God.   *(Philippians 1)*

Section 3

THE SUNDAY CELEBRATION

The Eucharist or Mass

You can make your Baptism more and more alive by coming each week to join the Christian family in celebrating the Eucharist together. So we are going to take a look now at what happens each week at Sunday Mass.

Coming together as God's people

When we come to Mass, we come to meet Jesus in two ways. First he comes to us through the Word of God and then he comes to us through the Bread and Wine.

Before we listen to the readings from the Bible, we prepare ourselves to hear them in the right way. We prepare ourselves to hear the Word which God speaks to us.

These are some of the things we do to prepare ourselves to hear the Word of God:

Pray quietly before the Mass begins.
Sing a hymn of praise to God as the Mass begins.
Ask God to forgive us for hurting one another.
Sing the "Lord, have mercy".
Sing the "Glory to God in the highest".

- *In your notebook write down* a prayer you might say quietly to yourself before the Mass begins.

- *Find the words of a hymn of praise that you know and look carefully at them.* What is the hymn thanking God for? Why is it important to start the Mass by saying "thank you"?

- *Look in a Missal to find the words that we use to ask God to forgive us.* Why is it important to say "sorry" at the beginning of the Mass?

- The "Lord, have mercy" and the "Glory to God in the highest" are songs of praise for God's love and forgiveness. *Look in a Missal to find these songs.* They are sometimes known by their Greek and Latin names. Can you find these names in the Missal?

The Word of God

When you became a catechumen you became a learner. You started to learn the Christian story. You were given a Bible and you began to learn the stories about Jesus and the stories that Jesus told and also the stories about the people of the Old Testament who waited so long for the coming of Christ.

As a Christian you always remain a learner. All your life you go on learning about Jesus. All your life you need to listen to those Bible stories.

And so when we come together each week at the Mass or Eucharist we listen to the WORD OF GOD from the Bible. Just as the friends of Jesus listened to his stories when they sat at table with him, so we also listen to his words. We listen to the words of Jesus just as if he was speaking straight to us.

First reading

The first reading is usually from the Old Testament. It tells us something about the story of the Jewish people before the time of Jesus. The first reading is often chosen to help us understand the Gospel reading better.

Psalm

After the first reading there is a psalm. This is a song of praise and prayer to God which comes from the Old Testament. The psalms are very ancient prayers. They were written as songs and so we often sing the psalm.

Second reading

This usually comes from one of the letters that were written to help the first Christians. These letters are full of advice about growing more like Jesus.

Gospel

Then the Gospel is proclaimed. This is where we hear the words of Jesus and the stories about Jesus. Often we sing an "Alleluia" before the Gospel is read. This is a greeting to Jesus who speaks to us in the Gospel.

The homily

Sometimes it is difficult even for grown-ups to understand what we hear in the readings. It is difficult to know what it all means for us today. And so we have a homily which helps to explain the readings and helps us to understand better what Jesus is saying to us now.

- Find *a Missal which gives the readings for next Sunday. Look first at the Gospel reading.* Do you know this story about Jesus? Even if you do know it, read it again. What do you think the story tells us about Jesus? What do you think is the most important thing it says?

- *Now look at the first reading.* Can you find any link between the Gospel and the first reading? What does the first reading teach you about God?

- *Look at the psalm.* Can you find one sentence in the psalm which you can make into your own prayer?

- *Look at the second reading.* See if you can find this same reading in your Bible. Sometimes the second reading can be very difficult to understand, but sometimes it is quite simple. What is this one like? Can you understand it?

- If you had to give the homily, what would you say about these readings? What message do you think they have for you and your friends?

The Creed

The Creed is a short summary of all the things that Christians believe. Let us remind ourselves of some of the things we learnt in the first part of this book and then see if we can find them in the Creed.

- We learnt that we know God as the FATHER, the SON and the HOLY SPIRIT.
  Where can you find the Father, the Son and the Holy Spirit in the Creed?

- We learnt that Jesus loved us so much that he was not afraid to die for us. We learnt that God's power was so strong in him that death could not hold him. We learnt that after three days Jesus rose from the dead.
  Where does the Creed talk about Jesus dying and rising again?

- We learnt that, as Christians, we must work and pray for the coming of God's kingdom.
  Where does the Creed talk about the kingdom?

- We learnt that we cannot be Christians alone but that we need one another in the Church.
  Where does the Creed talk about the Church?

- We learnt about Mary, the mother of Jesus, whose faith gave Jesus to the world.
  Where can you find Mary mentioned in the Creed?

By saying the Creed together each Sunday we remind ourselves of our Baptism. We remind ourselves that we have become:

Children of God the FATHER
who are able to grow more like JESUS the SON
through the power of the HOLY SPIRIT
who lives in us
and that we are members of the
Christian family
which is the CHURCH.

The prayers

After the Creed we pray for the needs of the Church and the world. This part of the Mass changes each week as we pray for different needs and different people.

- Why is it important that we pray together for other people during the Mass?

- If you were writing the prayers for next Sunday's Mass, whom would you pray for?

- Sometimes the prayers take up an idea in the readings. We ask God to give us the faith or love or trust that we have just heard Jesus talking about in the Gospel. As a rule the intentions centre around: the needs of the Church; the public authorities and the salvation of the world; those oppressed by any need; the local community. Can you use next Sunday's Gospel to help you write a prayer?

Try writing a set of prayers for next Sunday's Mass in your notebook.

A sacrifice of praise

Bringing our gifts

The OFFERTORY is the part of the Mass where we bring the bread and wine to the altar.

We bring what we have.

We give thanks that God has already given us this bread and wine.

We believe that God will take the small thing we have brought and let it become the special bread and wine which brings us closer to Jesus and to one another.

Find John chapter 6 in your Bible and read verses 5 to 14.

• Who brought a small thing in this story? What did he bring?
• Who gave thanks for this small gift?
• What did God do with this small gift?

Look in your Missal to find the words the priest says to give thanks for the bread and wine.

- Who shared in making this bread and wine? How?
- At the Offertory we sometimes collect money and bring it to the altar. Why do you think we do this?
- What else do we offer to God along with the bread and the wine?

The Eucharistic Prayer

This is the long prayer in which we give thanks to God for all God's goodness to us from the very beginning of creation. We remember the last supper which Jesus shared with his friends and we ask God to let this bread and this wine be for us the body and blood of Christ.

Find one of the Eucharistic Prayers in your Missal.

- Can you find the words the priest uses to give thanks to God for all God's goodness.

- What are the words we say or sing to join in this prayer of thanksgiving?

- Can you find the words the priest uses to ask the Holy Spirit to come upon these gifts of bread and wine?

- Can you find the words which tell us about the last meal Jesus shared with his friends?

- What do we say to show we believe that Jesus is with us?

- What other people are mentioned in this prayer?

At the end of the prayer we all say AMEN. This is sometimes called "the Great Amen". When we say AMEN at the end of this prayer, we are saying "yes" to everything that the priest has said. We are agreeing that this prayer is our prayer. We are all giving thanks to God for his goodness.

We all remember the last meal that Jesus shared with his friends. We all pray that the Holy Spirit will make our small gifts holy and special. We all believe that Jesus is with us now as we share together in the bread and wine.

Eating together in peace

Preparing for Communion

Before we receive Communion we all join together in saying the OUR FATHER, the family prayer. We remember that we belong to one another because we all call God "Father". We pray together for the coming of God's kingdom and we pray for the strength to help build that kingdom.

Then we offer one another a SIGN OF PEACE. This is another sign that we come to God together and that the communion which brings us close to Jesus also brings us close to one another.

Then the priest invites us to come and share in this supper in which Jesus feeds us with his own life. We answer:

> "Lord, I am not worthy to receive you, but only say the word and I shall be healed."

Find Luke chapter 7 in your Bible and read verses 1 to 11.

- Can you see where our prayer comes from?
- Who was healed in this Gospel story?
- Why do we pray to be healed as we come to Communion? What prevents us from being in communion with Jesus and with one another?

A sign for the world

At the end of the Mass the priest blesses us in the name of the FATHER and of the SON and of the HOLY SPIRIT. He sends us out to live *with* and *for* Jesus in our everyday lives. He sends us out to work and pray for the coming of God's kingdom.

The Eucharist does not end when we leave the church building. It goes on through ordinary lives which are lived with thanksgiving and trust in God.

If we live the Eucharist in our homes and at school and at work and at play then we will become a sign of hope for the world. We will help to carry the life of Jesus into the world and we will share with him in building the kingdom of God.